UN PEACEKEEPING.
PAST LESSONS AND FUTURE PROSPECTS

The Rt Hon Malcolm Rifkind QC, MP
Secretary of State for Defence

Annual Public Lecture
Department of Public International Law
University of Edinburgh
10 March 1995

THE DAVID HUME INSTITUTE

1995

FOREWORD

This is the text of a lecture given by the Secretary of State for Defence, Malcolm Rifkind, in the Department of Public International Law, University of Edinburgh, in March 1995. The lecture formed part of a programme celebrating the fifty years' existence of the United Nations. Mr Rifkind surveys the ways in which the role of the UN has changed in recent years following the end of the Cold War. As he aptly comments, there is a paradox in the way in which the confrontation of superpowers has been replaced by regional rivalries and tensions, often of a ferocious nature. Mr Rifkind describes the British contribution to the development of the UN's functions in this new situation, and analyses the lessons being learnt for further development in the future. He argues that the British input has been and continues to be vital, and underlines a commitment to maintaining what has already been achieved. The lecture provides both a fascinating picture of the current situation in global peacekeeping, where the press of events can make it hard to distinguish the wood from the trees, and an insight into the way in which current and future British policy is being formed. Although The David Hume Institute takes no view on the subject-matter of Mr Rifkind's discourse, we may be confident of the importance of what he has to say.

Hector L. MacQueen
Executive Director
April 1995

UN PEACEKEEPING -
PAST LESSONS AND FUTURE PROSPECTS

Introduction

I am pleased to have the opportunity this evening to give this lecture about UN peacekeeping operations, the lessons we have learnt and my perspective of future prospects.

To put this in context, perhaps I can start by reminding you that there have been more UN peacekeeping operations launched in the last six or so years than in the previous forty years. And this has not just been a growth in numbers; the complexity too has increased. In the UN's first forty years, the number of troops involved in UN operations peaked at a little over 20,000; and in practice was rarely more than half of that. Towards the end of last year, over 75,000 troops were deployed, from 76 nations, serving in 16 different operations. The UN now has larger forces carrying out tasks ranging from humanitarian aid and assisting refugees, to public administration and conducting elections, in addition to more traditional peacekeeping.

In fact, we have a paradox where the end of the Cold War has been both cause and effect. International affairs are no longer conducted in terms of confrontation between Superpower Blocks. The threat of conflict that hung over most of the last half-century has been removed. The UN is now free to take the more active role in the international community which its founders envisaged.

But the changes that have swept across the world have a grimmer side. The end of the Cold War lifted the lid on a range of suppressed rivalries, some of extraordinary bitterness. This has been compounded by the advanced and powerful weapons which are now widely available. This potential for instability transcends national disputes and national frontiers to become a problem for us all.

British Contribution

The United Kingdom has always contributed to UN operations. We have been long standing supporters of peacekeeping: the United Kingdom has provided a contingent with UNFICYP in Cyprus, where British personnel patrol the Nicosia sector of the buffer zone, for some thirty years. The United Kingdom has contributed signallers to Namibia, military observers to MINURSO (Western Sahara), and mine clearance training experts and naval monitors to Cambodia where UNTAC broke new grounds in terms of the complexity of its operations.

We now have some 3,900 personnel serving with the UN - in Cyprus, the Iraq/Kuwait border, Rwanda, Georgia and Bosnia. Some 3,600 more are on operations in support of UN Security Council resolutions in Iraq and former Yugoslavia.

Last year, we deployed some 600 personnel to Rwanda. Technicians from the Royal Electrical and Mechanical Engineers literally got UN operations on the road by repairing large numbers of unroadworthy UNAMIR vehicles. Our contribution was crucial. A field ambulance was able to provide medical care to returning refugees, and a field squadron from the Royal Engineers rebuilt bridges and repaired roads. Logistics specialists also played a vital role supporting the force as a whole. In fact, the British contingent filled a critical gap until longer-term logistic arrangements could be established. This form of rapid, fixed-term deployment, is one to which British forces are particularly well suited. I shall say more about this later.

We also contributed ships and a small training team to the US-led multi-national force in Haiti last year. Last week, HMS EXETER was involved in the multi-national Naval Task Group which covered the withdrawal of the UN peacekeeping forces from Somalia.

Current Commitment

Apart from Cyprus, UN operations in which British forces are currently involved include staff officers in Rwanda, military observers in Georgia, observers on the Kuwaiti border, and over 500 personnel to implement the No-Fly Zones over Iraq, where Harrier and Tornado aircraft are helping to monitor the Iraqi repression of the Kurds in the North and the Shia Marsh Arabs in the South. UN Security Council Resolution 688 condemned Iraq's repression of its civil population and insists that Iraq allow access by international humanitarian organisations to all those in need of assistance. Iraq has persistently failed to comply with this Resolution.

In former Yugoslavia, some 3,490 personnel are deployed with UNPROFOR and there are some 3,100 more British personnel on operations in support of the UN's Security Council Resolutions in the area. UNPROFOR's mandate is to protect innocent civilians caught up in the conflict. British forces play a pivotal role in helping to achieve that aim. They provide military escorts to humanitarian aid convoys and carry out ceasefire and other monitoring tasks to help create and sustain conditions on the ground which will allow the international diplomatic effort towards an overall peace settlement to continue.

In fact, as I discovered during my visit to Bosnia in December, hostilities in Central Bosnia have largely ceased at least for the time being. The people living there have, during the past year, begun to develop confidence in the Federation and the fragile peace that exists. They are beginning to return to something which has some resemblance to a normal life. They are rebuilding their homes, their children are returning to school, and basic amenities such as water, heat, light and sewage disposal are gradually being restored. Without the presence of UNPROFOR, none of this would have been possible. Indeed, British and other forces have been actively involved in these projects.

There has been considerable speculation in recent weeks about the possibility that UNPROFOR may have to be withdrawn. In Croatia we were very disappointed by President Tudjman's refusal to renew the UN Mandate. I sincerely hope that it may be possible to reach agreement with him on a continuing UN presence. Without that, I believe that there is a serious risk of renewed fighting, with consequential risks for other parts of former Yugoslavia and, indeed, the Balkan region as a whole.

In Bosnia, our aim must be to prevent the outbreak of renewed fighting, after the current Cessation of Hostilities Agreement expires at the end of April, to provide the environment in which a political search for a just and lasting settlement can continue.

In recent days you will have seen press reports about the possibility that the UK might send a force to Angola. The UN Security Council has voted to deploy a force - UNAVEM - to monitor the ceasefire which has now been achieved in Angola and to assist the peace process there. We have agreed in principle to meet a UN request to send a logistic battalion, of about 600 personnel, for a three-month period. This would set up the logistic infrastructure for the UN operation, and then hand it over to contractors who would be engaged by the UN.

This ceasefire represents a chance for peace in a country which has been ravaged for many years by a bitter civil war. UNAVEM III will play a vital part in making this work. If the operation is going to get off the ground promptly, and operate effectively, good logistics are vital. A British logistics battalion would, therefore, make a central contribution.

But the mounting of the operation, and our contribution to it, also depends critically on the willingness of both parties in Angola to demonstrate their good faith by meeting their obligations under the peace process. This includes a continued ceasefire and provision of airfield and other facilities needed by the UN force. Before we can make any final decision to commit a British force, therefore, we shall need to be certain that these obligations will be met.

Lessons of Peacekeeping

Turning to the lessons we have learnt from our long involvement in peacekeeping, British expertise in this field is now both widely acknowledged and respected. Our experience has given us a sharper insight into the nature of these operations, and we have learnt from experience. While the title of my lecture is "UN Peacekeeping", in fact the UN engages in a number of quite separate and different operations including peacekeeping, peacemaking, and, even, peace enforcement, collectively known as peace support operations. All our experience leads us to the view that there are two principal categories. The first, peacekeeping, comprises operations *with the consent of the parties* in support of efforts to achieve, or maintain, peace. The second, peace enforcement, encompasses operations to restore peace between parties who *may not consent* to intervention. The former are usually predicated on the existence of a ceasefire, and a longer-term political process which peacekeeping can assist.

But I should not pretend that it is always possible neatly to divide operations into these two categories. Reality is usually much harder to categorise. Tidy definitions which are useful for military planning can mean very different things for the forces deployed on the ground, and have different implications for the forces involved. There is a world of difference between patrolling the Green Line in Cyprus and the UN's operations in Bosnia, although both fall under the same broad label of peacekeeping. In Bosnia, the level of violence is very much higher. Indeed we had to deploy sophisticated armoured vehicles to support humanitarian relief operations, and there is general acceptance of the principle that our troops there may need to open fire with quite heavy weapons if that becomes necessary to defend themselves. In Bosnia, we have used cannon and heavy machine guns as well as small arms fire; the Danes have used main battle tanks.

It is, therefore, obvious that a spectrum of responses to potential or actual crises is clearly needed, starting with preventative diplomacy and running through humanitarian operations, traditional peacekeeping - i.e. operations to separate and monitor opposing groups after an agreed ceasefire, to large scale involvement by the international community to impose a settlement to a conflict. In the real world, these levels of response may, of course, overlap, e.g. a prophylactic military deployment to stabilise an area while preventative diplomacy is still underway, or, as in Bosnia, both humanitarian and peacekeeping operations.

The crucial distinction, however, is whether those involved in operations anywhere along this spectrum retain impartiality. In essence, this boils down to whether they are there with the consent of all the parties involved, or only some - or even none - on the other. Consent in this context does not, of course, mean that forces deployed with the consent of all sides will be free of accusations of bias - as we have seen in Bosnia - or that there may not be occasions when they need to defend themselves. There may well be attempts to manipulate them and their neutrality may not always be respected.

But there is at least acceptance in principle that they are not one of the parties to the conflict.

Without the consent of the parties, UN operations become substantially more complicated. The forces involved will not be regarded by all parties as impartial and, therefore, it will be almost impossible for them to revert to a neutral role at a later stage. They also lose the relative protection that neutrality provides. They will, therefore, probably have to use force, not merely in self defence but to impose a solution. They, therefore, risk becoming a party to the conflict they have been deployed to resolve.

These problems are exacerbated in civil wars. It is very hard for either the UN itself or the forces on the ground to determine who is victim and who aggressor. In these circumstances, the potential for very long, and, ultimately, inconclusive involvement by the UN grows. It also raises difficult questions of the rationale in international law for action by the UN, which are not present in conflicts between states.

I am not, in highlighting these difficulties, suggesting that we should never be involved in operations that do not have the consent of all parties. We should not, however, underestimate their difficulties and complexities. I believe, therefore, that operations in which the UN remains impartial should be the norm.

Defining the Task

That said, the nature of an operation can - and often does - change as a situation develops. Bosnia started as a humanitarian operation, has increasingly taken on a peacekeeping flavour, and there has been pressure from many sources for the UN to move to peace enforcement.

This raises the very difficult question of how to define, from the outset, the nature of each task, and, therefore, the forces that will be required for its successful completion. The forces that are required for one purpose may, simply, not be fit for another. We, therefore, seek a clear mandate, acceptable to all troop contributors, which spells out what they are there to do and the limits on the action that they can take before planning is finalised. We must recognise that, however clear the initial mandate, it will not be immune from political pressures created by changes in the circumstances on the ground, or, indeed, from public expectations that this may be neither well-informed nor even rational. In the jargon of the Ministry of Defence, this is known as "mission creep".

The next stage in defining the task is to ensure that the mandate is achievable. This may well influence the scope of the task undertaken; as American forces found in Haiti, explaining the limits of an operation brings its own difficulties. If, however, we do not agree an achievable mandate, there is a significant risk that the operation will not merely fail, but quite possibly that it will make matters worse and discredit the organisation sponsoring it. In this context, events in Mogadishu have presented some bitter lessons. There is general concern in the UN that its failure in Somalia has undermined its credibility as an organisation; and that this may deter nations from contributing to future operations. This concern would, I believe, be greatly exacerbated if the UN had to withdraw from either Croatia or Bosnia.

The process of defining a mandate may, therefore, affect the ability of the UN rapidly to deploy forces on an operation. But we ignore it at our peril. Similarly, the need to establish clear objectives against which to measure the success of the operation and, where possible to set a firm end date, is also vital. This, as in Cambodia, may take the form of a time limit on the operation as a whole, or on the duration of individual nations' contributions. The prospect of an open-ended deployment - of the type we have become accustomed to in Cyprus - is a deterrent to potential troop contributors. We believe that it is much better to establish from the outset the principle of rotation between troop contributors so that individual nations can be confident of a finite commitment.

As with many other aspects of UN operations, enunciating this principle is rather easier than putting it into practice! However clearly we may define the objectives of an operation and the timetable for achieving them, it can be very difficult to pull out if the underlying problem has not been solved. No matter how much hard realism points to cutting our losses, political factors and public opinion frequently pull in the opposite direction.

Public Opinion

This brings me to the role which public opinion can play in determining both whether a UN operation is mounted and, in particular, whether individual nations contribute. In political terms Governments can face uncomfortable choices. They have a responsibility to satisfy themselves that military involvement is an appropriate response to a crisis; and that forces, once deployed, have an acceptable prospect of succeeding in accomplishing the tasks they have been set. It may, therefore, be necessary to decide in some circumstances against military involvement. But doing this can be extremely difficult when domestic, and international, opinion is strongly of the view that "something must be done".

Public opinion can create a huge surge of support for involvement in particular operations, and the media is very influential in shaping this opinion. For understandable reasons, the media focuses on bad news. In complex conflicts, it is also difficult within the constraints in which journalists operate to portray a balanced picture which properly represents all the factors in a conflict. The public see harrowing scenes of genuine need and react equally genuinely with demands for action. The problem is that it is not always so easy to identify what that action should be.

As in the Gulf conflict, Western publics have seen the remarkable power and sophistication of the equipment operated by their armed forces. What they may not readily appreciate is that, in peacekeeping, some of this capability may be neither appropriate nor useable within the mandate for the operation or without destroying what we are seeking to preserve. In peacekeeping operations - as opposed to peace enforcement - the use of force is strictly limited to the minimum required for self defence. The forces are not deployed to influence the course of the conflict itself. That is why, in Bosnia for instance, there are limits on the use of overwhelming airpower. This can be difficult for public opinion to accept.

I also want to make one more point before I leave this section on public opinion. That is that the public desire that "something must be done" may not be sustained if involvement in a bitter conflict in a country in which no vital national interests are at stake results in casualties. The clamour for action can turn, almost overnight, into an equally vigorous clamour to "bring our boys home". And the Government cannot afford to ignore the need for public support for British involvement in UN operations.

UN Peacekeeping Capabilities

I have tried to set out the increasingly complicated background against which the UN has to operate. Given the very rapid growth of UN operations, its resources have inevitably been stretched; and, post the Cold War, there are likely to be more and more occasions when the UN is called upon to act. It is, therefore, examining how it can enhance its capacity to plan and launch peacekeeping operations. In 1992, the Secretary General published his report "An Agenda for Peace", which identified a number of areas where UN capabilities could be increased. The UK welcomed this report and continues to take an active part in the debate it fostered, particularly to identify practical measures which will bolster the UN's capabilities. We recognise the need for the UN to improve its command, control, and planning abilities. If it is to be able to react flexibly to swiftly changing circumstances, the best approach would be to create a General Staff, comprising civilian and military, who could provide the necessary core for strategic planning for peacekeeping operations. It would principally work in New York to an agreed professional doctrine, but it might also provide personnel to deploy in the early stages of operations to put the plans developed into operation. Such a Staff would augment the existing embryonic planning and operations cell, and provide a much needed injection of capacity, expertise, and experience.

In our view, this should be allied to clearer, unified command and control arrangements. The UN Headquarters should concentrate on strategic planning, for which a General Staff would give a capability, and on the political direction to the UN command in the field. The latter's role is to undertake the detailed operational planning and assign individual tasks to the forces in the field. This is, however, in practice a difficult area where political sensitivities are complicated by individual nations' understandable desire to have a say in what tasks their contingents are asked to undertake.

But I would not wish you to get the impression that the picture is all gloomy. Progress has been made. The Planning Staff in New York is being enhanced and we seconded British Service personnel to the UN. They have played an especially prominent part in establishing a Situation Centre to act as the UN's eyes and ears, by monitoring developments in trouble spots around the world and sifting information from operations in progress. The Secretary General, himself, has taken the welcome decision to simplify UN command arrangements by amalgamating the Department of Peacekeeping Operations and the field operations division.

Our positive reaction to "An Agenda for Peace", was followed up by a well received and constructive response to the standby force planning initiative which emerged from it. This seeks to overcome the problem of delays in deploying personnel when a peacekeeping operation is launched. We are maintaining a dialogue with the UN team which is leading on this work; and to assist them, have given them substantial information on the capabilities and readiness of UK forces which are potentially available for peacekeeping.

This brings me to the doctrine for such operations. A common peacekeeping doctrine would undoubtedly assist the integration of contingents from different countries within a UN force. The British Army has been prominent in the developing thinking in this area. A new Army manual - "Wider Peacekeeping" - has been produced after widespread consultation. It encapsulates thinking which is increasingly accepted by a large number of troop contributors, and it will, I hope, be very influential.

Force Contributors

In addition to the changes in the UN's management and organisation which I have described, the upsurge in the level of peacekeeping also raises the question of where the forces can be found. There have been suggestions that the UN should have a standing capability or forces earmarked for peacekeeping. Circumstances will, of course, vary from country to country but the Government's perception is that earmarking specific troops is not the answer to the UN's problems. It is extremely difficult to forecast in advance exactly what capabilities will be needed for each operation or which nations will be acceptable; this leads to a high risk of a mismatch between the forces earmarked for the UN and its actual needs. Our preference is to ensure that the UN has a clear view of the capabilities we have to offer, and to consider our contribution on a case-by-case basis.

A standing UN force also has problems. Few Governments are likely to give the UN *carte blanche* over the deployment of their forces. A directly raised force would have to face the difficulty of ensuring that it had - and maintained - the wide, and growing, range of capabilities likely to be required now - and in the future - for peacekeeping operations, and of keeping personnel current in a full spectrum of skills and doctrines. Current operations also require highly trained troops who have the discipline and confidence to avoid the pitfalls of over-reaction in the face of provocation. Our belief is that the best starting point for this is well-trained personnel who have the experience of general military service with their own national armed forces.

Balancing Commitments

I have set out the developments in the UN's thinking and capabilities to mount peacekeeping and other peace support operations. I now want to turn to the question of the circumstances in which British personnel should be involved. In taking such a decision, we need to balance commitments and resources. Like most nations, we have considerable freedom to decide the number and type of forces we wish to commit. But although choice brings freedom, it also brings responsibility. As a permanent member of the Security Council, we wish to play a significant part, and are doing so. But we cannot do everything. As the Foreign Secretary has said on previous occasions, there are times when we will have to say no. We need, therefore, to satisfy ourselves first that military involvement is the most appropriate response to a problem; and, secondly, to balance our involvement against other commitments, available resources, and our foreign policy objectives.

The Future Prospects

I should now like to turn to the future. I believe there is every likelihood of a continuing demand for peacekeeping, and I hope that the UN will be able to continue the process it has begun of enhancing its own capabilities. I can assure you that the Government intends to continue to play an active part in these developments. In particular, we would like to see early progress in the further development of the UN planning mechanism into a peacekeeping General Staff to plan future operations and establish a common UN peacekeeping doctrine. Continued work to improve command and control arrangements are also important, but I recognise this is a complicated issue and is not likely to be resolved quickly.

These improvements are vital because the UN is the only truly world-wide organisation which has the authority to legitimise military action by the international community, and significant experience and expertise in the field of peacekeeping. It must, therefore, have primacy in this area.

I am not, however, arguing that regional organisations do not have a useful role to play under a UN Mandate. The recent Franco-British initiative on African peacekeeping is a good example of this. We are seeking to build on existing mechanisms for early warning and the traditions of preventative diplomacy, to help African States enhance their ability to deploy forces on peacekeeping operations. We are proposing that peacekeeping "skills centres" could be established in African staff colleges; that logistic bases could be established under UN control to store equipment; and that other countries could assist through training and short-term logistics advisory teams.

NATO, the Organisation for Security and Cooperation in Europe, the European Union and Western European Union, can also contribute in their different ways to identifying and forestalling conflict; and can conduct peacekeeping operations where necessary. A great deal of work is being done to adapt these organisations to these new challenges. NATO resources are already being used alongside the UN in Bosnia - for sanctions enforcement in the Adriatic, in conjunction with WEU; elements of NATO Mobile Headquarters are incorporated in UNPROFOR Headquarters; NATO AWACs aircraft provide data to UN commanders; and NATO provides the aircraft to enforce the No-Fly Zone and provide close air support for UNPROFOR. Wider assistance, including NATO command structures, would be used if withdrawal from Bosnia becomes necessary. While Bosnia is the first theatre in which NATO forces have been used for UN peacekeeping operations, I do not believe that it will be the last. NATO and WEU are already learning from the problems which the ad hoc arrangement for deployment in and around former Yugoslavia created. This has significantly affected the work currently underway in NATO to develop Combined Joint Task Forces, which could operate under either NATO or WEU auspices.

Finally, I want to turn to a very important development in the way in which the British Services might contribute to UN operations. I spoke earlier about the perennial problems of getting forces on the ground without delay at the start of an operation. Nations such as the United Kingdom whose armed forces have a well-developed, rapid deployment capability naturally are the first ones to which the UN look in these circumstances. But there is a natural reluctance to enter into an open-ended commitment. We are, therefore, looking at whether short-term deployments to hold the ring while an operation gets underway, and then hand over to contingents from other nations should be the norm. Our involvement in Rwanda was time limited in this way and we envisage that a deployment to Angola would follow the same pattern.

Peroration

Since the end of the Cold War, the theory and practice of UN peacekeeping has developed substantially; and it is continuing to develop. I can see no slackening in the demand for the UN's good offices, and the UK will continue to be a major participant in its operations. The skills and professionalism of British Service personnel deployed on UN operations are widely and justly acknowledged. I pay tribute to this; they have had a distinguished role in the UN's history.

The Government is determined that this distinguished record will be maintained, and we shall continue to discharge our responsibility as a permanent member of the Security Council. We now need to build on the progress that has been made in both the theory and practice of UN operation, and we shall continue to work to enhance the UN's capacity to plan and mount them.

I cannot pretend that it will always be possible to predict where crises will erupt; but I can say with certainty that they will. The United Kingdom, and the British armed forces in particular, will continue to play its part as a responsible member of the Security Council in the eternal endeavour for international peace and stability.

The David Hume Institute

The David Hume Institute was registered in January 1985 as a company limited by guarantee: its registration number in Scotland is 91239. It is recognised as a Charity by the Inland Revenue.

The objects of the Institute are to promote discourse and research on economic and legal aspects of public policy questions. It has no political affiliations.

The Institute regularly publishes two series of papers. In the **Hume Paper** series, now published by Edinburgh University Press, the results of original research by commissioned authors are presented in plain language. **The Hume Occasional Paper** series presents shorter pieces by members of the Institute, by those who have lectured to it and by those who have contributed to 'in-house' research projects. From time to time, important papers which might otherwise become generally inaccessible are presented in the **Hume Reprint Series**. A complete list of the Institute's publications follows.

Hume Papers

1   Banking Deregulation (out of print) *Michael Fry*
2   Reviewing Industrial Aid Programmes:

    (1) The Invergordon Smelter Case *Alex Scott and Margaret Cuthbert*
3   Sex at Work: Equal Pay and the "Comparable Worth" Controversy *Peter Sloane*
4   The European Communities' Common Fisheries Policy: A Critique *Antony W Dnes*
5   The Privatisation of Defence Supplies *Gavin Kennedy*
6   The Political Economy of Tax Evasion *David J Pyle*
7   Monopolies, Mergers and Restrictive Practices: UK Competition Policy 1948-87 *E. Victor Morgan*

Published by Aberdeen University Press

8   The Small Entrepreneurial Firm
    Gavin C Reid and Lowell R Jacobsen
9   How should Health Services be Financed? *Allan Massie*
10 Strategies for Higher Education—The Alternative White Paper
    John Barnes and Nicholas Barr

Books

The Deregulation of Financial Markets
edited by Richard Dale, Woodhead-Faulkner, London, 1986

Governments and Small Business
Graham Bannock and Alan Peacock, Paul Chapman, London, 1989

Corporate Takeovers and the Public Interest
Graham Bannock and Alan Peacock, Aberdeen University Press, 1991

Social Policies in the Transition to a Market Economy: Report of a Mission to the Russian Federation organised by the United Nations January 1992
Michael Hay and Alan Peacock, Alden Press, Oxford, 1992

Hume Reprints

1   The 'Politics' of Investigating Broadcasting Finance *Alan Peacock*

2   Spontaneous Order and the Rule of Law *Neil MacCormick*

3   Governance and Accountability: Corporate Governance *J.C. Shaw*

Further details of publications may be obtained from:

The Secretary, The David Hume Institute, 21 George Square, Edinburgh EH8 9LD, Tel 0131-650 4633: Fax 0131-667 9111.